About the Sacraments

Les Miller

NOVALIS

© 2011 Novalis Publishing Inc.

Cover design: Mardigrafe
Cover illustration: Anna Payne-Krzyzanowski
Interior images: pp. 7, 25, 30, 35, 45: Plaisted; pp. 12, 18, 39: W.P. Wittman
Layout: Mardigrafe and Audrey Wells
Reviewed by Heather Reid

Published by Novalis

Publishing Office
10 Lower Spadina Avenue, Suite 400
Toronto, Ontario, Canada
M5V 2Z2

Head Office
4475 Frontenac Street
Montréal, Québec, Canada
H2H 2S2
www.novalis.ca

Library and Archives Canada Cataloguing in Publication

Miller, Les, 1952-
    25 questions about the sacraments / Les Miller.

Issued also in an electronic format.
ISBN 978-2-89646-375-6

    1. Sacraments--Catholic Church--Juvenile literature. 2. Catholic Church--Doctrines--Juvenile literature. I. Title. II. Title: Twenty-five questions about the sacraments.

BX2200.M55 2011   j264'.0208   C2011-904232-0

Printed in Canada.

All rights reserved. No part of this publication may be reproduced, stored in a retrieval system, or transmitted in any form, or by any means, electronic, mechanical, photocopying, recording, or otherwise, without the written permission of the publisher.

The Act of Contrition used in Question 22 is found in *A Catechesis on Reconciliation*, Canadian Conference of Catholic Bishops, 1995.

We acknowledge the financial support of the Government of Canada through the Canada Book Fund for business development activities.

5   4   3   2   1   15   14   13   12   11

TABLE OF CONTENTS

A WORD FROM THE AUTHOR... 5

WHERE SACRAMENTS COME FROM 6
1. What are the seven sacraments?.............................. 6
2. What's so sacred about the sacraments? 8
3. What do the sacraments have to do with Jesus? 9

THE SACRAMENTS OF INITIATION................................. 11
4. What happens at Baptism?...................................... 11
5. What is the meaning of water and
   the other symbols of Baptism?................................ 13
6. Why do we baptize babies?..................................... 15
7. What is confirmed at Confirmation? 16
8. What happens to a person at Confirmation?............. 18
9. Why is Confirmation often celebrated at Pentecost?.. 20
10. What is the meaning behind some of the rituals
    and symbols at Confirmation?................................. 21
11. Why is the Mass also called the Eucharist? 23
12. Why is the Eucharist so important to Catholics?....... 24
13. What difference does the Eucharist
    make in a person's life? 26
14. How often should I go to Mass? 27

25 Questions... About the Sacraments

THE SACRAMENTS OF VOCATION 28

15. Why is Marriage a sacrament? 28
16. What is the meaning behind some of the rituals and symbols at a wedding? 29
17. What does the Catholic Church teach about divorce? 31
18. Who can receive the sacrament of Holy Orders? 32
19. What happens when a person receives the sacrament of Holy Orders? 34
20. Why are only men allowed to be priests in the Roman Catholic Church? 36

THE SACRAMENTS OF HEALING 37

21. Why are Catholics expected to celebrate Reconciliation? 37
22. What do I do when I celebrate the sacrament of Reconciliation? 38
23. How do I deal with my embarrassment at going to confession? 41
24. What is the purpose of the sacrament of Anointing of the Sick? 43
25. How is the sacrament of Anointing of the Sick celebrated? 44

WORDS TO KNOW 46

A Word from the Author

I became a member of the Catholic Church when I was an adult, so I vividly remember celebrating my first sacraments: Baptism, Reconciliation, Eucharist, and Confirmation. These were very special moments for me because I felt very close to God.

Do you remember your First Communion? Have you celebrated your Confirmation? Chances are these moments were a big deal in your family. You probably got dressed up for the occasion and may even have had a party with family and friends afterwards. As we grow older, we understand that there is much more to the sacraments than nice clothes and festivities. The more we know about the sacraments, the more we can discover how God speaks to us in these important events.

It is natural to have questions about what is happening in the sacraments. This book tries to answer some of these questions. The sacraments draw us close to God, but we can't properly explain God in words. One of the earliest Greek words for sacrament means "mystery." That's because the sacraments bring us into contact with the mysterious love of God. No human words can describe exactly how God is at work in the sacraments, but my hope is that this book will guide you further down the road of deeper understanding of these wonderful and powerful meetings with God.

Les Miller

WHERE THE SACRAMENTS COME FROM

What are the seven sacraments?

The seven sacraments of the Catholic faith are important celebrations that connect believers with God. These are Baptism, Confirmation, Eucharist, Marriage, Holy Orders, Reconciliation (Penance), and Anointing of the Sick.

Sometimes we divide them into categories: sacraments of initiation, sacraments of vocation, and sacraments of healing.

- A process called *initiation* introduces people into a group. We call Baptism, Confirmation and Eucharist the *sacraments of initiation* because through them, new Catholics are welcomed into the faith.

- When we figure out what God is calling us to do in our lives, we have discovered our *vocation*. Marriage and Holy Orders are *sacraments of vocation*.

- When we need to mend our relationship with God and others, we celebrate the sacrament of Reconciliation. When our bodies are sick, we can ask for healing in the Anointing of the Sick. These two sacraments are the *sacraments of healing*.

All the sacraments are important religious *rituals*. Rituals are actions that have a deep meaning. For example, the ritual of making the sign of the cross is about more than moving our hands in a pattern. The cross reminds of the death and resurrection of Jesus and identifies us as Christians. Sacraments contain many different rituals. For example, Baptism involves pouring water, anointing with oil, blessing the person who is being baptized, clothing them in a white garment, and recognizing them as the light of Christ.

In the Bible, Jesus tells us that we must love God and love our neighbour just as we love ourselves. These "three loves" are found in the seven sacraments. They connect us with God, with each other and with our deepest self. In Confirmation, we make promises to God, our neighbours and ourselves. These promises help us to be more loving.

 The number seven is found often in the Bible. For example, the story of Genesis (the first book of the Bible) describes the creation of the world as lasting seven days. Also, Jesus asked us to forgive seventy times seven times. The number seven is a symbol of completeness and God's perfection. We will explore the symbolism of numbers in more detail in *25 Questions about the Bible*.

25 Questions... About the Sacraments

What's so sacred about the sacraments?

People often feel close to God at key moments in their lives. We celebrate birth in Baptism, growth in Confirmation, our life choices in Marriage and Holy Orders, our moments of healing in Reconciliation and Anointing of the Sick, and our ongoing loving friendship with God in the Eucharist. The sacraments are moments when we can be very close to Christ.

Sacraments are more than events. They are celebrations! These ritual celebrations contain symbols and actions with deep meaning attached to them. The more we understand their meanings, the better we will see how Christ is with us at these special times. Sacraments are also "the masterpieces of God," as the *Catechism of the Catholic Church* tells us (#1116).

The sacraments are sacred because they bring us close to God. God's love and power is called *grace*. This warm and healing love is always reaching out to us as a gift. Sacraments are grace-filled celebrations. All the symbols and actions in the sacraments tell us about God's deep caring for us all.

One traditional definition of a sacrament is "an outward sign of an inward grace instituted by Christ." The *outward signs* include different parts of the celebration, such as the water at Baptism. *Inward grace* is God's love and power. *Instituted by Christ* means that these sacraments began with Jesus. In Question 3, you will find some scripture references that tell you where each sacrament can be found in the Bible.

> The word "sacrament" comes from the Latin word *sacrare*, which means "to make sacred." This is a translation of the ancient Greek word *mysterion*, or "mystery." Both meanings express our belief in God's presence in the sacraments.

> Grace is a gift we can't earn through our actions. God gives it to us freely! We can't convince God to love us, because God already loves us. And we can never fully repay God's gift. God gives us the gift of life and the gift of his Son to show us the way we are to live our lives.

3

What do the sacraments have to do with Jesus?

Jesus lived a fully human life 2,000 years ago in the Holy Land. How can we deepen our love and friendship with someone who lived so long ago and so far away? Jesus Christ is also fully divine, the Son of God. How can we have a relationship with God, whom we can't see or touch? Catholics believe that the deepest way we meet Jesus in our lives is through the sacraments.

- When we celebrate Baptism, we remember the Baptism of Jesus in the Jordan River. (Mark 1:9-11)
- When we celebrate Confirmation, we remember the Holy Spirit coming upon Jesus at his Baptism and upon the disciples and Mary at Pentecost. (John 16:7, Acts 2:1-4)
- When we celebrate Eucharist, we remember the many meals Jesus shared with his followers, especially the Last Supper, held the night before he died. (Matthew 26:26-28, Mark 14:22-24)
- When we celebrate Marriage, we remember how Jesus blessed the wedding at Cana with his first miracle. (John 2:1-11)
- When we celebrate Holy Orders, we remember how Jesus called on his disciples at the Last Supper to celebrate the Eucharist in his memory. (Luke 22:20)
- When we celebrate Reconciliation, we remember the many times that Jesus forgave (even on the cross) and taught forgiveness through parables, such as the story of the prodigal son. (Luke 15:11-24, John 20:21-23)
- When we celebrate Anointing, we remember Jesus healing the sick. (Mark 6:12-13)

We will explore each of these connections more deeply in the remaining questions.

> At Pentecost, the Holy Spirit came upon the disciples and Mary in the form of tongues of fire over their heads. For more on this amazing event, read the Acts of the Apostles, chapter 2. You will find it in the New Testament of the Bible, after the Gospel according to John.

> In the parable of the prodigal son, the father forgives his son after the son leaves home and wastes a great deal of the family fortune. This wonderful story is found in the Gospel according to Luke, in the New Testament.

THE SACRAMENTS OF INITIATION

What happens at Baptism?

This answer describes a typical Baptism of a baby, but of course some people are baptized as adults. The priest or deacon presides at the celebration of this sacrament, which normally takes place near the doors of the church, around the baptismal font. The font is a large basin or

25 Questions... About the Sacraments

bowl that holds the water that is used for baptizing. The font is placed near the church doors to remind us that one of the meanings of Baptism is welcoming people into the Church. A priest or deacon leads the celebration, and all the worshippers, including parents, godparents, family members and parishioners, are witnesses. Often Baptism is held as part of Sunday Mass.

The priest or deacon welcomes and blesses the worshippers. He invites parents and godparents to trace the sign of the cross on the baby's forehead. This is a reminder that we belong to Christ. The parents are asked what they want for their child. They answer, "Baptism."

They then make promises based on the words of the Apostles' Creed. These promises summarize the faith of the Church. They agree to raise their child according to the teachings of the Catholic Church.

The priest or deacon pours water over the baby's head or immerses (dips) the baby in the font of water, saying, "I baptize you in the name of the Father, and of the Son, and of the Holy Spirit." Everyone responds by saying, "Amen!"

A small baptismal candle is lit for the child from the large Paschal candle. The baby is sometimes given a white garment to put on. Blessing prayers are then said.

- The Easter candle or Paschal candle is lit for the first time at the Easter Vigil. It represents the light of the risen Christ among us.

- A deacon can preside at Baptisms and weddings. He is a minister of the Church and often helps the priest at Mass and serves God's people in other ways as well.

- Godparents agree to support the parents of the baptized baby as they raise their child in the Catholic faith.

5

What is the meaning of water and the other symbols of Baptism?

The water, oil, candle and white garment used in Baptism all have deep spiritual meanings. The *font* or basin of water contains holy water. This specially blessed water is poured over the person being baptized. Sometimes the person is immersed (dipped) in this water. This is no ordinary water! Every year, the water is blessed at the Easter

Vigil: the priest prays a special prayer and then plunges the bottom of the Paschal candle into it. Water is a powerful symbol from both the Jewish and the Christian traditions. God saved Noah from the flood. The Israelites were freed from slavery in Egypt by passing through the waters of the Red Sea. Jesus was baptized in the River Jordan. Water is a symbol of life. Without water, we could not survive. We also use water to cleanse our bodies. In Baptism, water is a symbol for cleansing our souls.

The priest or deacon makes the sign of the cross on the person's forehead and chest with the oil of chrism, which is made of olive oil and balsam. Olive oil represents the grace of God and sweet-smelling balsam represents goodness or virtue. Chrism (which comes from a Greek word that means "anointing") is a symbol for sealing the person with the gifts of the Holy Spirit. (We will explore the gifts of the Holy Spirit in Question 7.)

A small baptismal candle is lit from the tall Paschal or Easter candle. The Easter candle represents Jesus, who is called the "light of the world" in John's Gospel. Baptism celebrates not only new life but also a dying to old ways that do not lead to God. The candle is a guide to this new life. It reminds us that long after the celebration is over, we will always belong to Christ.

The person being baptized wears a white garment at Baptism. White is the colour of purity and innocence. It tells us that at Baptism we are blessed by God and are loved very much.

A supply of holy water is made available for the Church community for the rest of the year. When we bless ourselves with the water found in the shallow bowls (called stoups) as we enter the church, we are using holy water.

Churches are given the oil of chrism at a special Mass held at the local cathedral, usually during Holy Week. They also receive the oil of the catechumens and the oil of the sick at this time.

Why *do we baptize babies?*

In the early days of the Church, most of the people to be baptized were adults, because they had to decide for themselves to join the followers of Jesus. Later, most of those who became members of the Church did so when they were babies. Their parents made this decision for them.

There were good reasons for infant Baptism. First, Baptism is seen as a ritual of welcoming someone into the community of God's love. We want everyone to belong to the Church, so how could we say that babies and children could not be members just because they were young? Also, Baptism is a sacrament where we celebrate God's love, which is stronger than sin. Baptizing babies celebrates the action of Jesus, which offers people the way to a deeper relationship with God. The sooner that relationship begins, the better.

> St. Augustine taught that Baptism washed away the original sin that was handed down to us by Adam and Eve. They were forbidden from eating the fruit that would give them special knowledge, but they ate the fruit anyway because they wanted to be like God. Baptism washes away that original sin to bring us closer to God.

What is confirmed at Confirmation?

When we confirm something, we make sure that it is true. For example, we can confirm with our teacher that a test really will be held on Friday. In the sacrament of Confirmation, we celebrate the confirming of the Spirit given at our Baptism. At Baptism, if we were baptized when we were young children, our parents and sponsors make the promises for us. At Confirmation, we renew those promises ourselves. We were anointed with the oil of chrism at Baptism. At Confirmation, we are anointed with this same oil as we deepen our relationship with God. Grace is God's love for us.

Confirmation used to be celebrated at Baptism. (Remember that in the early Church, most people coming into the Church were adults.) Most Christian communities had a Bishop who led the part of the celebration that became our sacrament of Confirmation. As the number of Christians grew, the Bishop was not able to get to all the Baptisms. To get around this problem, priests and deacons began to celebrate Baptisms, but the Confirmation part of the ritual was not done until the Bishop could be there. Over time, Baptism and Confirmation became two separate sacraments in the Latin Rite, which Roman Catholics follow.

Children can be confirmed as young as five years old, but for many reasons, a bishop may decide to celebrate Confirmation at a later age in his diocese. He can also give the local parish priest the responsibility of confirming young people.

 In the Eastern Catholic Churches, priests were given the right to confirm those entering the Church. These new members of the community were baptized, confirmed and given communion in the same celebration. This practice continues today with young children who are welcomed into the Eastern Church.

What happens to a person at Confirmation?

In Canada, most young people are confirmed between ages of seven and 15. They prepare for the sacrament with others who will celebrate Confirmation so they can learn more about it. The more they know about this ritual, the more they can appreciate its beauty and power. The person being confirmed is called a confirmand. Confirmands are asked to choose a sponsor who is a confirmed and practising Catholic

and is usually 16 years old or older. The sponsor supports the young person in his or her spiritual life. Having a sponsor is a reminder that the Christian life is not just about our relationship with God, but also about our relationship with others. A sponsor is like a godparent at Baptism.

The rite of Confirmation takes place at Mass, after the homily. During this ritual, those being confirmed are presented to the Bishop (or the priest). The confirmands renew their baptismal promises. The key moment in the ritual comes when the Bishop (or priest) anoints the confirmands with the oil of chrism. First he places his hands on the person's head to call the Holy Spirit upon him or her. Then the Bishop (or priest) anoints the person, saying, "Be sealed with the gift of the Holy Spirit."

Here are the parts of the rite of Confirmation:
- The calling of the confirmands
- The homily
- The renewal of baptismal promises
- The laying on of hands
- The anointing with chrism
- The thanksgiving prayer after Confirmation

Why is Confirmation often celebrated at Pentecost?

At the Jewish feast of Pentecost, the disciples and Mary were gathered in an upper room in Jerusalem. They didn't know what to do when Jesus was no longer with them. Jesus had promised to send the Holy Spirit to guide them, but they were still waiting. Suddenly, the Spirit came upon them as tongues of fire above their heads and as a great gust of wind. The community of disciples was inspired and given gifts to continue along the way that Jesus had taught them.

Christians celebrate the feast of Pentecost, too. Pentecost is seen as the birth of the Church. Confirmation is connected to Pentecost because the confirmands are also sealed with the gifts of the Holy Spirit given at Baptism. Those confirmed are strengthened with grace to do God's work. Confirmation is the second sacrament of initiation, so it is usually celebrated in the Easter season.

There are seven gifts of the Holy Spirit:

- *wisdom* to act guided by faith, hope and love
- *understanding* to see the world with caring eyes
- *right judgment* to make good decisions

25 Questions... About the Sacraments

- *courage* to do the right thing
- *knowledge* about how God's love is at work in the world
- *reverence* for all that is good and holy
- *wonder and awe* at the magnificence and power of God and God's creation.

> Sometimes the gift of wonder and awe is called "fear of the Lord." This phrase tells us that Christians should be humble before God's presence and respect God's great power.

> If you want to find out more about Pentecost, read chapter 2 of the Acts of the Apostles in the Bible. It is an amazing story!

What is the meaning behind some of the rituals and symbols at Confirmation?

During the ritual of Confirmation, the Bishop places his hands on the confirmand's head. *Laying on of hands* is an ancient Christian ritual for calling upon the power of the Holy Spirit. Jesus laid his hands on the sick to heal them and to pass on his powerful grace. In the early Church, authority was passed from one leader to another using a similar ritual. Laying on of hands also takes place during the sacrament of Holy Orders, which we will look at in Question 19.

Then the Bishop or priest traces the sign of the cross with the oil of chrism on the forehead of the one being confirmed and says, "Be sealed with the gift of the Holy Spirit." This is the same oil that is used at Baptism. It is made of olive oil and balsam and has been blessed by the bishop. The person responds, "Amen." (So be it!)

At a celebration of the sacrament of Confirmation, you will see the colour red in the church. The Bishop or priest will wear red vestments and you may see artwork showing tongues of flame used in decorations. Red is the colour usually associated with Pentecost. It is the colour of flames and is often associated with the Holy Spirit, which came as tongues of fire over the heads of the disciples and Mary as they waited in the upper room at Pentecost.

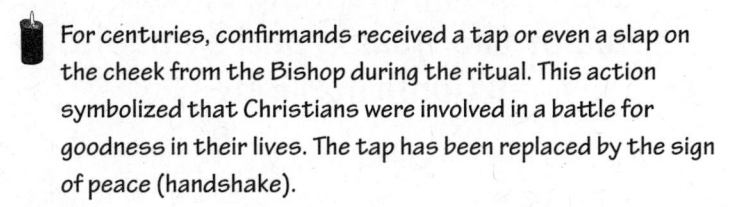

> For centuries, confirmands received a tap or even a slap on the cheek from the Bishop during the ritual. This action symbolized that Christians were involved in a battle for goodness in their lives. The tap has been replaced by the sign of peace (handshake).

> Our baptismal name is the one normally used in the Confirmation liturgy. In a few places, those being confirmed

25 Questions... About the Sacraments

choose a Confirmation name, which is the name of a saint or other holy person. The aim of this extra name is to connect the person being confirmed with someone who is a model of Christian living for them.

Why is the Mass also called the Eucharist?

The Mass has four parts: the Introductory Rites, the Liturgy of the Word, the Liturgy of the Eucharist, and the Concluding Rites.

The word "Mass" comes from the Latin word *missa*, which means "sent." Until about 50 years ago, Mass around the world was celebrated in Latin. At the end of the liturgy, the priest said, *"Ite missa est,"* which means "Go, it is the dismissal." These words asked people to bring the gifts and graces they had received at Mass into their daily lives. The origins of the word "Mass" do not capture the entire meaning of the celebration, but they do speak of our mission to complete the prayers of the Mass by living good lives.

The word "Eucharist" comes from a Greek word that means "thanksgiving." Thanksgiving or expressing gratitude is a very important part of Mass, but this word doesn't capture the full meaning either. The Eucharist is the sacrament of love that Jesus gave us at the Last Supper. (For more on the meaning of the Eucharist, see *25 Questions about the Mass*.)

> Communion is the part of the Mass when those who are gathered share the body and blood of Jesus Christ. This happens during the Liturgy of the Eucharist. The word "communion" comes from the same root words that give us "community." Communion is a deep union between the worshippers and God.

Why is the Eucharist so important to Catholics?

The Eucharist is sometimes called the central sacrament of Christianity. In this sacrament, we meet Jesus Christ in very special ways. We meet him in the Gospel (the word of God), in the people who gather in his name, and especially in receiving communion.

Many of the other sacraments are celebrated within the Eucharist, including Baptism, Confirmation, Marriage and

Holy Orders. Eucharist is the most frequently celebrated of all the sacraments. It is no wonder that the Church calls the Eucharist "the source and summit of the Christian life."

Eucharist gives us the spiritual strength to lead good and holy lives. Did you ever get inspired after watching a movie or a sports event? You want to be just like your favourite star. Mass is like that and more. When we are open to Jesus' love coming through the Eucharist, we are inspired to be people of joy, courage and justice.

> The word "inspired" comes from the word for "spirit." It is a good word to describe the action of Jesus working through us, because when that happens, we meet the Holy Spirit.

> In the Roman Catholic tradition, most young people celebrate their First Communion at around age seven, or what is called the "age of reason." This is a time when children are starting to make responsible decisions and have a deeper understanding. First Communion is the beginning of a lifetime of receiving the sacrament of the Eucharist. That is something to be celebrated!

25 Questions... About the Sacraments

What difference does the Eucharist make in a person's life?

Have you ever had a friendship with someone that brings out the best in you? Some of our friends help us to find qualities in ourselves that we didn't know we had. We are happier and kinder when we are with them. Building a friendship with Jesus not only brings out our best side but also makes us better than we could be without him. The love that comes from this friendship both guides us and strengthens us.

The Mass draws us together as a community. We are all together doing the same thing, worshipping God. The Mass is the glue that holds us together during good times and hard times.

The Mass is also a spiritual exercise. Physical exercise makes us stronger. Spiritual exercise helps us to live fuller lives as we follow Jesus. Going to Mass regularly gives us wisdom to make good decisions, compassion for those who are suffering, hope when we are worried about something, and the knowledge that God loves us.

 The *Catechism of the Catholic Church*, a book that contains the teachings of the Church, tells us the benefits or "fruits" of receiving the Eucharist.

a) It gives us a closer union with Christ

b) It deepens the grace we are given at Baptism

c) It cleanses us from past sins and restricts us from future sins

d) It strengthens unity among members of the Church, and

e) It renews our care for the poor. (#1391–1397)

How often should I go to Mass?

What's the point of having a friend if you don't spend time with them? Jesus is the best friend we could ever have, so it makes sense to gather with the community and worship him at Mass regularly. During Mass, we praise God together, listen to God's word, pray and sing together, and share in Christ's body and blood. That is why the Church says we are to go to Mass every Sunday and, in Canada, at Christmas and on the Solemnity of Mary, Mother of God (which is celebrated on New Year's Day). Of course, the Church encourages us to attend Mass more often if we can. Many people like to go to Mass during the week when it is a special day, such as a feast day, or if they want to remember someone who is sick or has died, or just because they need some spiritual support.

Going to Mass is one thing, but truly paying attention when you are there is another! Some people go to Mass and don't pay much attention to the words and rituals. When this happens, the Mass becomes a routine. A routine is something we do again and again without thinking about its meaning. (Brushing your teeth is a routine.) During the Mass, Jesus tells us in many ways that we are loved, so we need to pay attention. When we go to Mass, we need to be present in both body and spirit.

 In some countries, the people are asked to go to Mass on other special days as well. For example, in Italy, these include the feasts of Epiphany, Assumption, All Saints and the Immaculate Conception.

THE SACRAMENTS OF VOCATION

Why is Marriage a sacrament?

Choosing to get married is a very important decision. The person we marry is someone we love and trust completely. We also share a commitment to raise a family together and to serve those around us and follow Jesus.

The Catholic Church also says there should be a strong spiritual connection between a couple who is choosing to marry. This is why marriage is considered a sacrament. The bond between couples is a powerful symbol of God's love acting in the world. It is a sign of how Christ loves the Church and an eternal bond that cannot be broken. God's love and care shine through the marriage when the spiritual bonds are strong.

Of course, in every marriage there are times of disagreement and misunderstanding. Couples practise the virtues of faith, hope and love when they need to overcome these trials.

For the first few centuries, the Church did not consider marriage an official sacrament. As the Church came to understand the importance of marriage, it decided to recognize marriage as a sacrament.

What is the meaning behind some of the rituals and symbols at a wedding?

The sacrament of Marriage – or matrimony, as it is sometimes called – takes place at a church, either as part of the Mass or outside of Mass, as a separate ritual. Weddings are held at the church because the husband and wife's commitment needs the support of the whole community in their regular place of worship.

In Catholic sacraments, the minister is one who leads the worship. At Mass, the minister of the sacrament is the priest or deacon. At a Catholic wedding, the ministers are the couple who are getting married. The priest or deacon is the chief witness.

The main act of worship in the marriage ceremony is the exchange of vows or promises between the man and the woman. As part of this ritual, they exchange rings as a sign of their unending love. Many other customs are associated with marriages. In some cultures, the bride wears a white dress; in other cultures, the bride wears brightly coloured clothing. The part that does not change is the exchange of vows, which are promises of love and faithfulness for their life together.

What does the Catholic Church teach about divorce?

Divorce falls under the laws of the country, not the Church's laws. Only the courts of the nation can grant a divorce. Still, the Catholic Church discourages divorce. The Church teaches that a sacramental marriage cannot end because it is a symbol of Christ's love for his people, which is never-ending.

Unfortunately, some Catholic married couples cannot live together. If the marriage took place before the man and woman were mature enough to make such an important decision, or if one or both of them were forced to marry, or were mentally unstable, or lied about their marriage promises, Church authorities could recognize that a sacramental marriage never really took place. This process is called *annulment*. In the eyes of the Church, a marriage that was not a sacramental bond can be annulled.

In such cases, the man and woman can each marry again in the Church later on if they follow the other laws of the Church, such as going to Mass regularly and taking part in the sacrament of Reconciliation.

Whenever a marriage ends, there is emotional pain for the whole family. Everyone needs time to heal. Sometimes children feel hurt or even guilty when this happens. And some adults think that annulments make it seem that there was never a legal marriage. But the Church is not saying that the marriage was not legal, or that love was absent in that family, or even that love has ended. The Church is saying that the marriage was not sacramental.

The Church cares about families who go through a divorce. It teaches that God's love and care will help us through difficult times. At such times, we need to keep our friendship with Jesus alive and stay connected with our parish family.

18

Who can receive the sacrament of Holy Orders?

In the sacrament of Holy Orders, men become deacons, priests or bishops. Those who receive this sacrament have had a special call from God to take on this important role. To prepare to be leaders in the Church, they spend a number of years in prayer and study in a process called *discernment*. When they receive this sacrament, they are *ordained*.

A *deacon* is an ancient role that we read about in the Bible. Deacons and deaconesses were involved in baptizing new members of the Church. Today, deacons help the priest at Mass and serve God's people in other ways: offering spiritual care to the sick and their families in hospitals, to prisoners, to the elderly, to street people, and to others who need God's healing touch. Deacons must be men who are at least 35 years old. They may be married and have children.

A *priest* needs a great deal of spiritual training and study before he is ordained. Priests first receive what are called the *minor orders* while they study at a special school for priests called a *seminary*. Near the end of their training, they are ordained as deacons. Finally, they are ordained as priests at the end of their time in the seminary.

A *bishop* is a priest who is called to lead. He is the spiritual guide of the faithful in his area (called a *diocese*) and carries on the work of the early apostles, teaching and sharing the Gospel with others. An archbishop is a bishop of an archdiocese.

At the end of 2009, according to the Vatican, there were 410,593 priests in the world.

What happens when a person receives the sacrament of Holy Orders?

A priest receives the sacrament of Holy Orders during Mass in the presence of at least one bishop. Here is what happens:

a) Those being ordained (*ordinandi*) are called forward.

b) The bishop presents the ordinandi to the gathered assembly.

c) The members of the assembly agree that the ordinandi should become priests.

d) The final lesson and examination are given to the ordinandi.

e) The ordinandi promise obedience.

f) While the ordinandi lie face down on the floor, special prayers are said.

g) The ordinandi are given some of their priestly clothing.

h) The hands of the ordinandi are anointed with oil.

i) Gifts are presented.

j) A sign of peace is exchanged.

The last two actions are the most important:

k) The bishop lays his hands on the head of each ordinand; all the priests present do the same.

l) In a special prayer, the bishop asks the Holy Spirit to come upon each ordinand.

> In the fifth century, priests (and monks) would have the hair on the top of their scalp shaved off. This was called a *tonsure*. This practice lasted for many centuries.

> Other people, both men and women, take the vows of religious life without being ordained. These include religious brothers and sisters. They take vows to live in community as unmarried men and women, devoting themselves to God and serving God's people.

> The sacraments of vocation are sometimes called the sacraments of mission.

Why are only men allowed to be priests in the Roman Catholic Church?

In North America today, where women and men have equal rights, it may seem strange that only men are priests. Where did this practice come from?

The first place to look is in the Bible. When we look at the example of Jesus, we see that he had many followers, both male and female. Important women in the story of Jesus include Mary, his mother; his friends Martha and Mary; and Mary Magdalene, who was the first person to meet the risen Christ. But Jesus chose only men to be his apostles – his followers who were called to preach the Gospel after he rose from the dead.

The Church teaches that at Mass, the priest represents Christ for us, the assembly. Because Jesus was male, the Church thinks that the priest should also be male.

This practice is not meant to show that men are superior to women. In fact, women are greatly valued and are active in many ways within the Church. We even describe the Church as Holy Mother Church and the bride of Christ. Also, many Catholics are very devoted to the Blessed Virgin Mary, who shows us how to live lives of faith and love for God.

> The Roman Catholic Church's Latin Rite (the form that most Canadians practise) has a tradition of an unmarried priesthood. In the Eastern Catholic Rite, and some other Christian traditions, priests are allowed to marry.

THE SACRAMENTS OF HEALING

21

Why are Catholics expected to celebrate Reconciliation?

In our lives we have many choices. Most of the time we make good choices, but sometimes we make wrong decisions. Sinful actions aren't simply mistakes or accidents. Sins happen when we are aware that a choice we make will hurt our relationship with God, others or even ourselves. We can hurt our relationship with God by choosing to disobey one of the Ten Commandments or by ignoring the teaching of Jesus to love God and our neighbours as ourselves. We can hurt others by being deliberately cruel or by stealing. We can hurt ourselves by using drugs or alcohol. When our relationships are harmed, the sacrament of Reconciliation helps to heal them. That is why the Church teaches that we should celebrate this sacrament at least once a year. Celebrating our loving, merciful God is the most significant part of the sacrament.

> The Ten Commandments are found in the Old Testament in the Bible. You can find them in the Book of Exodus, chapter 20, verses 2 to 17.

> The sacrament of Reconciliation is also called the sacrament of Confession and the sacrament of Penance.

22

What do I do when I celebrate the sacrament of Reconciliation?

Before you go to the priest to confess, prepare yourself by remembering what you have done wrong. This process is called an *examination of conscience*. It will help you to focus on those things that harm your relationship with God and others. You can prepare a mental or even a written list of whatever you wish to confess to the priest.

Confessions take place in a private space, where no one else can hear you. In a church, this usually is a reconciliation room or a confessional. (See *25 Questions About What We*

See in a Catholic Church for more information on these two types of spaces.) Here is normally what happens when you take part in this sacrament.

a) Go into the reconciliation room or confessional. You may have a choice about having your confession face-to-face with the priest, or behind a screen. Think about which you would prefer.

b) Make the sign of the cross and say, "Bless me, Father, for I have sinned."

c) Say how long it has been since your last confession. For example, you might say, "It has been four months since my last confession."

d) Tell the priest your sins. Tell him if there is something that you do often (such as fight with your brother or sister) that you would like to stop doing. And tell him if there is something you did just once that is harming your relationship with God or with the people around you. You don't have to give a lot of details. The priest understands that we all do wrong at times and will help you to move forward.

e) Finish by saying, "For these and all past sins, I am truly sorry."

f) The priest will then give you some advice that can help you do better. He may give you penance to do. Your penance could be saying some prayers or doing something to help heal your relationship with God and others.

g) The priest may ask you to say an Act of Contrition, which is a prayer where you say you are sorry (contrite) for what you have done. For example, you might say, "God, I am sorry for all my sins: for what I have done and for what I have failed to do. I will sincerely try to do better. Help me to walk by your light. Amen."

h) The priest then gives you absolution. This means that your sins are forgiven! He gives absolution in the name of the Father, and of the Son, and of the Holy Spirit. While he is doing this, you make the sign of the cross and then say, "Amen."

i) The priest then says a short closing prayer.

j) Do your penance as soon as possible after your confession so you don't forget.

Some priests have their own style of celebrating this sacrament. Take your lead from the priest and ask questions if you are not sure what to do next.

> If you go to confession, you must be truly sorry for your sins and want to change your behaviour. This is called *contrition*.

> If you are nervous about going to confession, you can tell the priest that you need his help to say the right thing. He will be happy to help you.

23

How do I deal with my embarrassment at going to confession?

We are not proud when we do something wrong, so it is not surprising that we feel a little ashamed and embarrassed about telling someone our faults. But when we look at the sacrament more closely, there's no reason to feel awkward about confession. It is good to talk about our burdens in a sacred setting. Jesus healed many people during his lifetime. He continues his healing ministry in the sacrament of Reconciliation through the priest.

After all, we aren't confessing to just anyone. The priest is a special person because he represents Jesus Christ. God already knows our misdeeds as well as our good deeds. We confess to a priest because we need to tell the community about what we have done wrong. In fact, telling the whole community was the way that confession first took place in the early Church. Over time, the priest came to represent God and the community. When we confess to a priest, he uses his special training and spiritual insights to advise us how to deal with our sins.

You don't need to worry about the priest telling anyone else about what you say to him when you confess your sins. He makes a solemn promise not to tell anyone about what is said in confession. This is called the *seal of the confessional*.

> Celebrating Reconciliation regularly is a good spiritual practice. It helps us to heal our broken relationships with God and others. And, as in any sacrament, we receive God's love in a special way.

What is the purpose of the sacrament of Anointing of the Sick?

As Christians, we try to follow in the footsteps of Jesus by healing one another through our words and actions. When we are seriously ill, we need spiritual strength to deal with our sickness. In the sacrament of Anointing of the Sick, we celebrate the healing power of Jesus to bring us life, even though our bodies may be failing. How can this be? Our faith teaches us that the spiritual life continues after our bodies fail us and we die. Both our tradition and scientists tell us that spiritual health can lead to physical health. In this way, the sacrament of Anointing of the Sick can sometimes lead people towards physical healing in addition to spiritual healing.

Even if the person does not get better, this sacrament is important for their Christian life. Anointing of the Sick celebrates the forgiveness and healing power of Jesus in our lives.

People don't have to be close to death to be anointed. Although older people who are close to death often celebrate this sacrament, people of all ages who are having major surgery or who are very sick also may be anointed.

Often parishes celebrate this sacrament as a commuinty. The Church teaches that "as soon as anyone of the faithful begins to be in danger of death from sickness or old age, the fitting time to receive this sacrament has certainly already arrived"(*Catechism of the Catholic Church* #1514).

> In the letter of the Apostle James in the New Testament we read, "Are any among you sick? They should call for the elders of the church and have them pray over them, anointing them with oil in the name of the Lord. The prayer of faith will save the sick, and the Lord will raise them up; and anyone who has committed sins will be forgiven." (James 5:14-15)

25

How is the sacrament of Anointing of the Sick celebrated?

The celebration of this sacrament often involves just the priest and the person needing healing. It can take place at church, in the hospital, at home, or in any other suitable place.

During this sacrament, the person is assured of forgiveness for all their sins for which they are truly sorry. Because it involves this sacramental forgiveness, only a priest can celebrate this sacrament with the person who is sick. He lays his hand on the person as a sign that he is calling upon the power of the Holy Spirit. The priest then takes the oil of the sick, which is olive oil that has been blessed by the Bishop. The priest anoints the person's forehead with the oil, saying, "Through this holy anointing, may the Lord in his love and mercy help you with the grace of the Holy Spirit." He then anoints the person's hands, saying, "May the Lord who frees you from sin save you and raise you up."

- At one time this sacrament was called *Extreme Unction* and was given only when a person was very close to death. "Unction" comes from the Latin word *unctio*, which means "to anoint."

- People can celebrate this sacrament more than once.

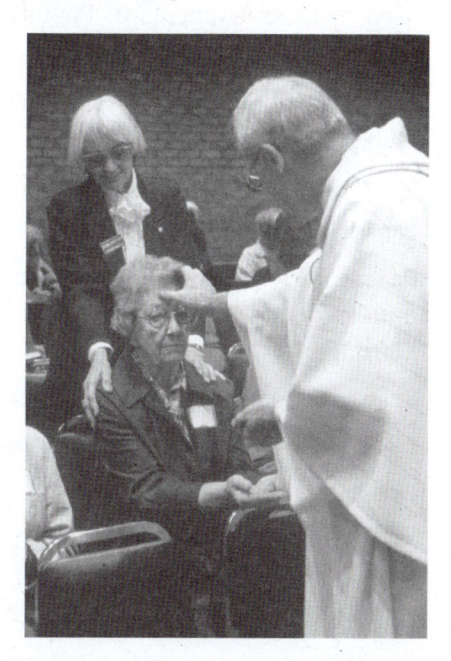

WORDS TO KNOW

Annulment: The process in the Roman Catholic Church for deciding that a couple did not have a sacramental marriage.

Anoint: To dab a person's skin with oil during a religious ritual.

Bishop: The leader of the Catholic community in a certain area, called a diocese.

Chrism: A special oil made from olive oil and balsam that is used in the sacraments of Baptism, Confirmation and Holy Orders.

Communion: The part of Mass when those gathered receive the body and blood of Christ.

Confirmand: A person who will receive Confirmation.

Contrition: Being sorry for one's sins.

Deacon: A person who receives Holy Orders, serves the community and can preside at the sacraments of Baptism and Marriage.

Diocese: The area under the care of the Bishop.

Discernment: A prayerful way of coming to a decision.

Examination of conscience: A way of looking at our life to see which decisions have hurt our relationships with God and with people.

Font: A large basin or bowl that holds the holy water used in Baptism.

Grace: God's love and power that constantly reaches out to us.

Initiation: The early stages of joining a group.

Laying on of hands: A ritual that is used to call on the power of the Holy Spirit.

Matrimony: Marriage.

Ordinandi: Those who are about to receive Holy Orders.

Pentecost: The coming of the Holy Spirit among the apostles and Mary after Jesus' ascension to heaven.

Reconciliation: Healing of broken relationships.

Ritual: Sacred actions that have a deep meaning.

Sacrament: A grace-filled ritual that brings us into a deeper relationship with Jesus Christ.

Seal of the confessional: The vow of secrecy that a priest takes. It means that the priest will not tell anyone what we say when we confess our sins.

Seminary: A place where men who are entering Holy Orders study and prepare for ordination.

Symbol: An object that has a deep and often spiritual meaning.

Tonsure: The top of a man's head that is shaved as a symbol that he is a priest or a monk.

Vocation: A calling to live your life according to God's dream for you.

Imprimé sur du papier Silva Enviro 100% postconsommation
traité sans chlore, accrédité ÉcoLogo et fait à partir de biogaz.